COLOURING TRACING

ACTIVITIES BOOK

BY

NORAH PERRY

This Book Belongs

To

NAME: ______________________________

CLASS: ______________________________

Date: Score:

Alphabet A to Z

Color the drawing and trace the word

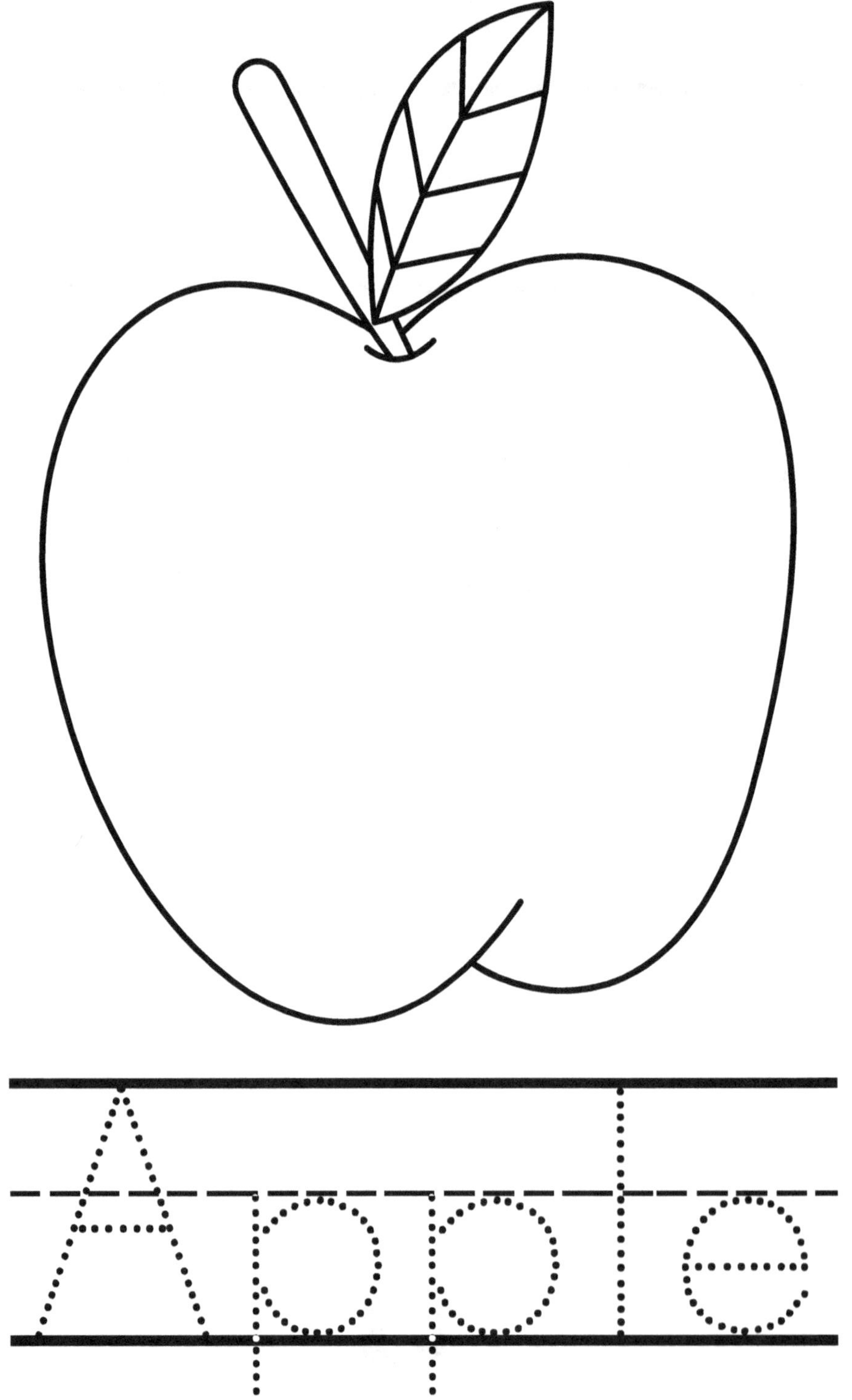

Score: ______________

Trace the letter

Trace the letter

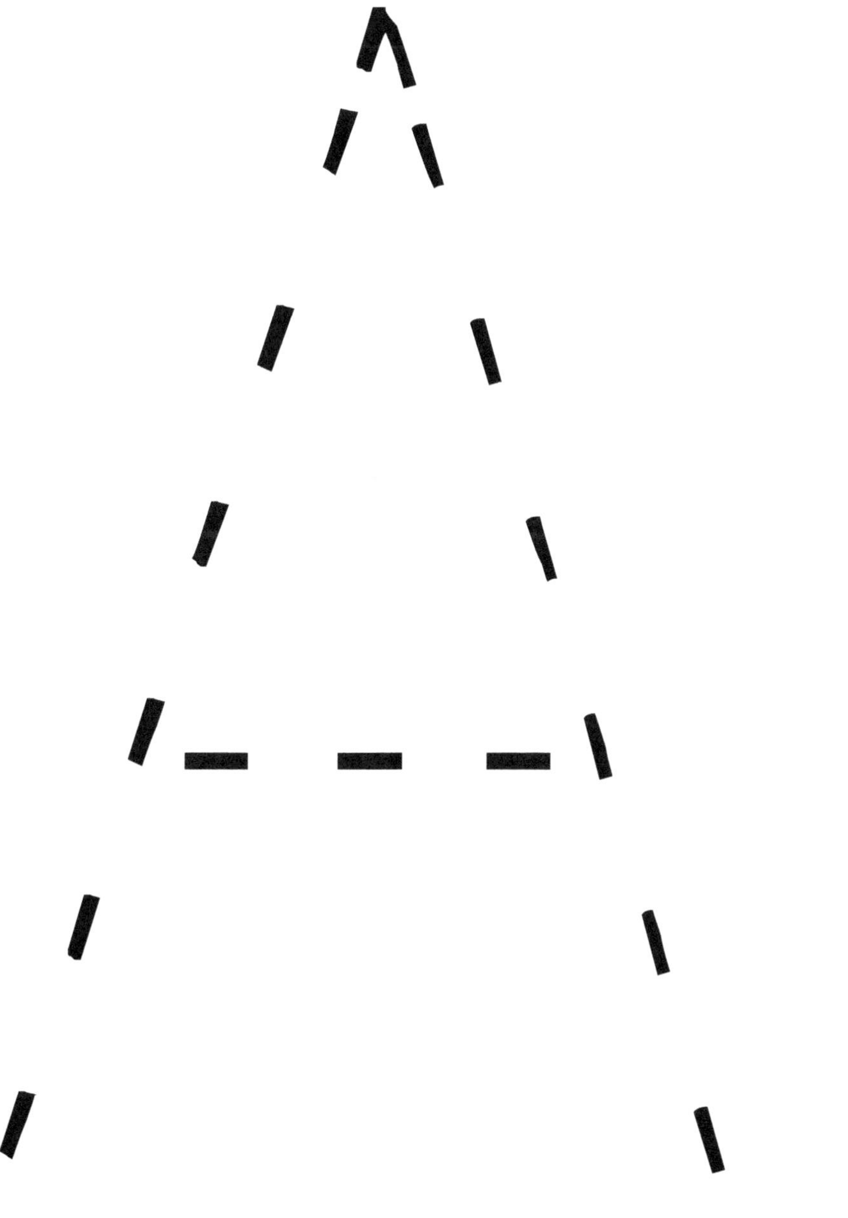

Date: Score:

Alphabet A to Z

Color the drawing and trace the word

Banana

Score: ____________

Trace the letter

Trace the letter

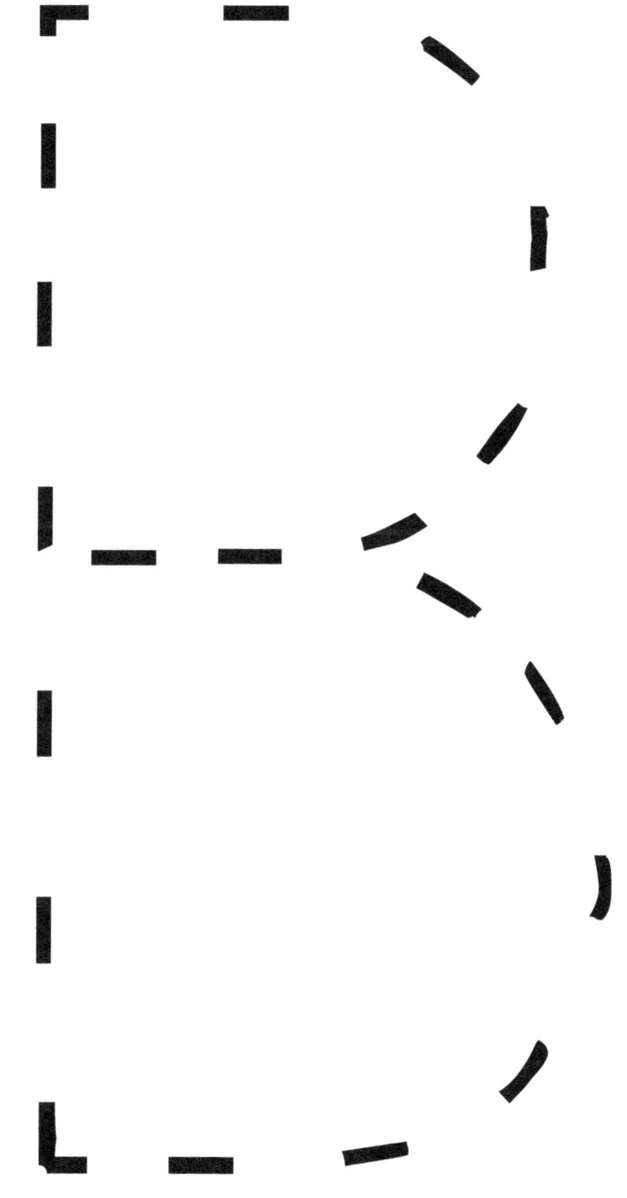

Date: Score:

Alphabet A to Z

Color the drawing and trace the word

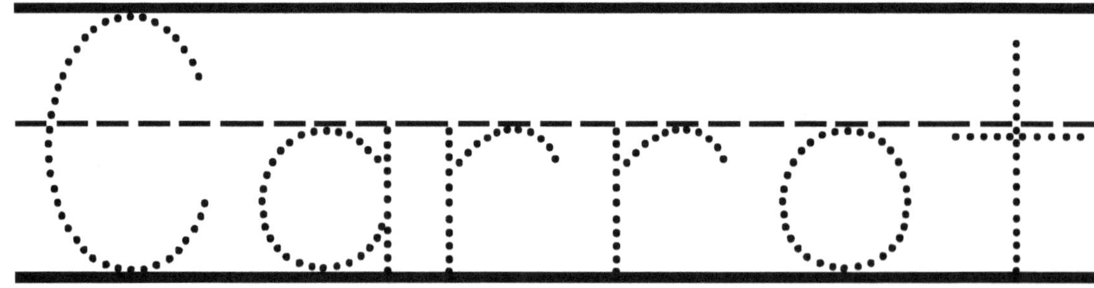

Score: ______________

Trace the letter

Trace the letter

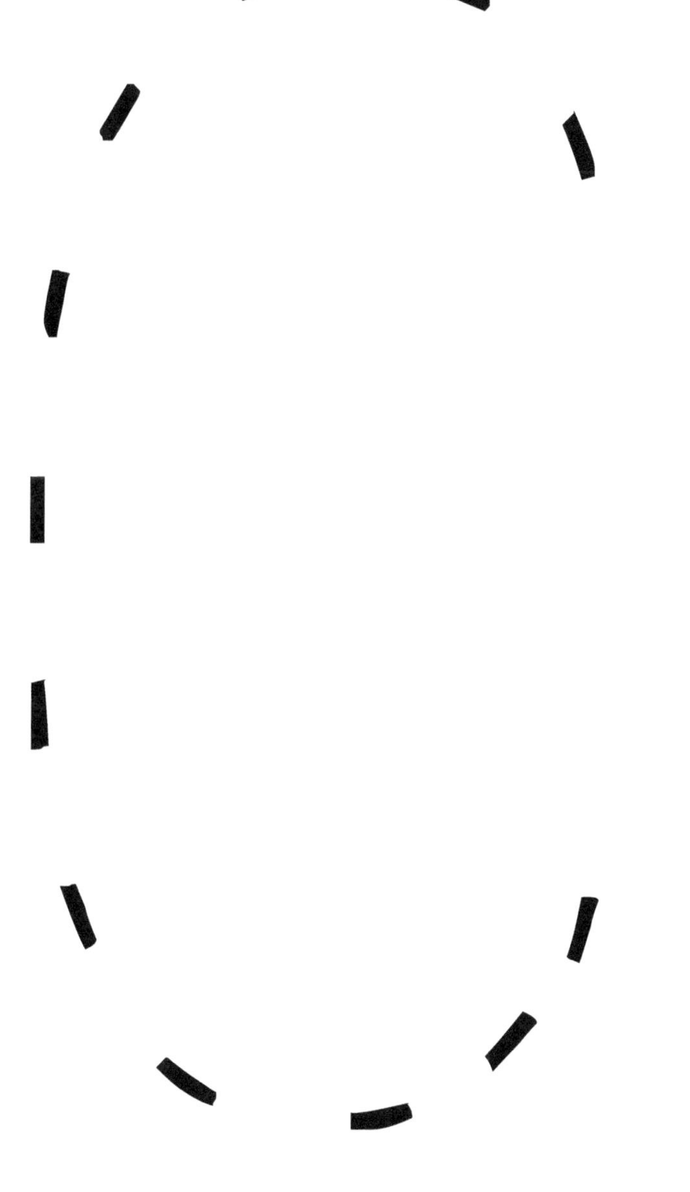

Date: Score:

Alphabet A to Z

Color the drawing and trace the word

Duck

Score: ______________

Trace the letter

Trace the letter

Date: Score:

Alphabet A to Z

Color the drawing and trace the word

Eggplant

Score: ____________

Trace the letter

Trace the letter

Date: Score

Alphabet A to Z

Color the drawing and trace the word

Flower

Score: ______________

Trace the letter

Trace the letter

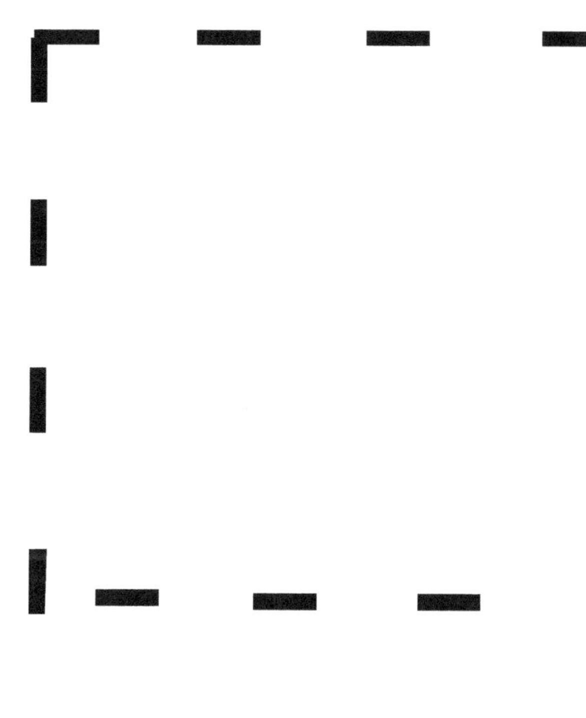

Date: Score:

Alphabet A to Z

Color the drawing and trace the word

Gift

Score: ______________

Trace the letter

Trace the letter

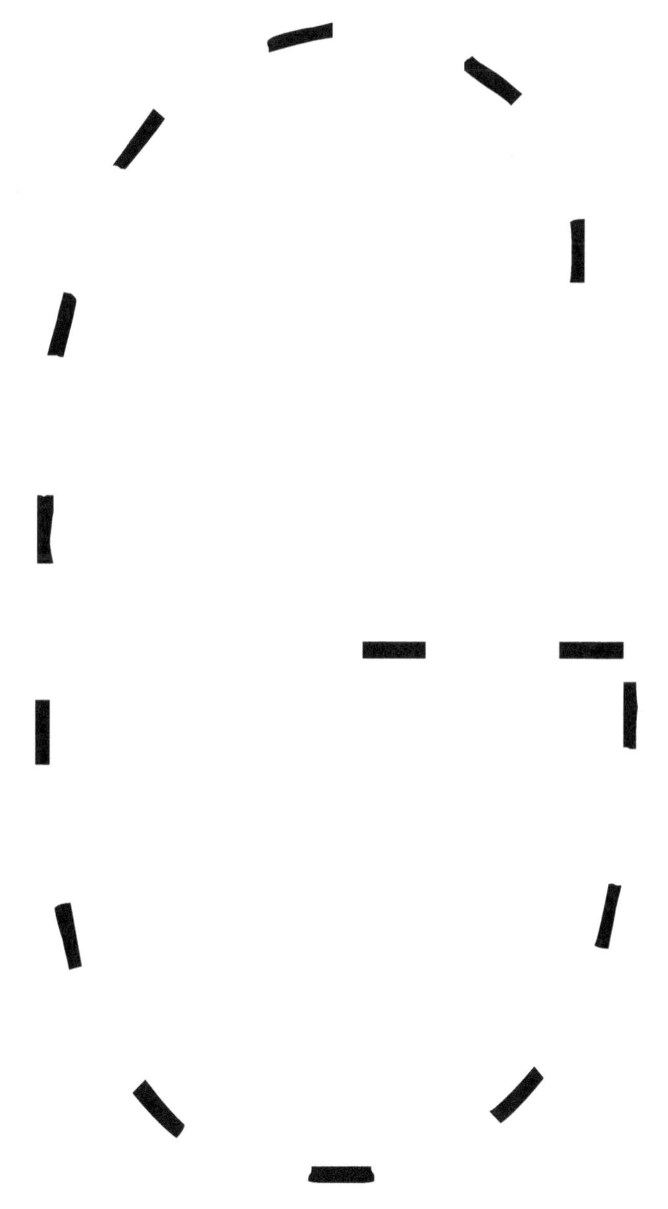

Date: Score:

Alphabet A to Z

Color the drawing and trace the word

House

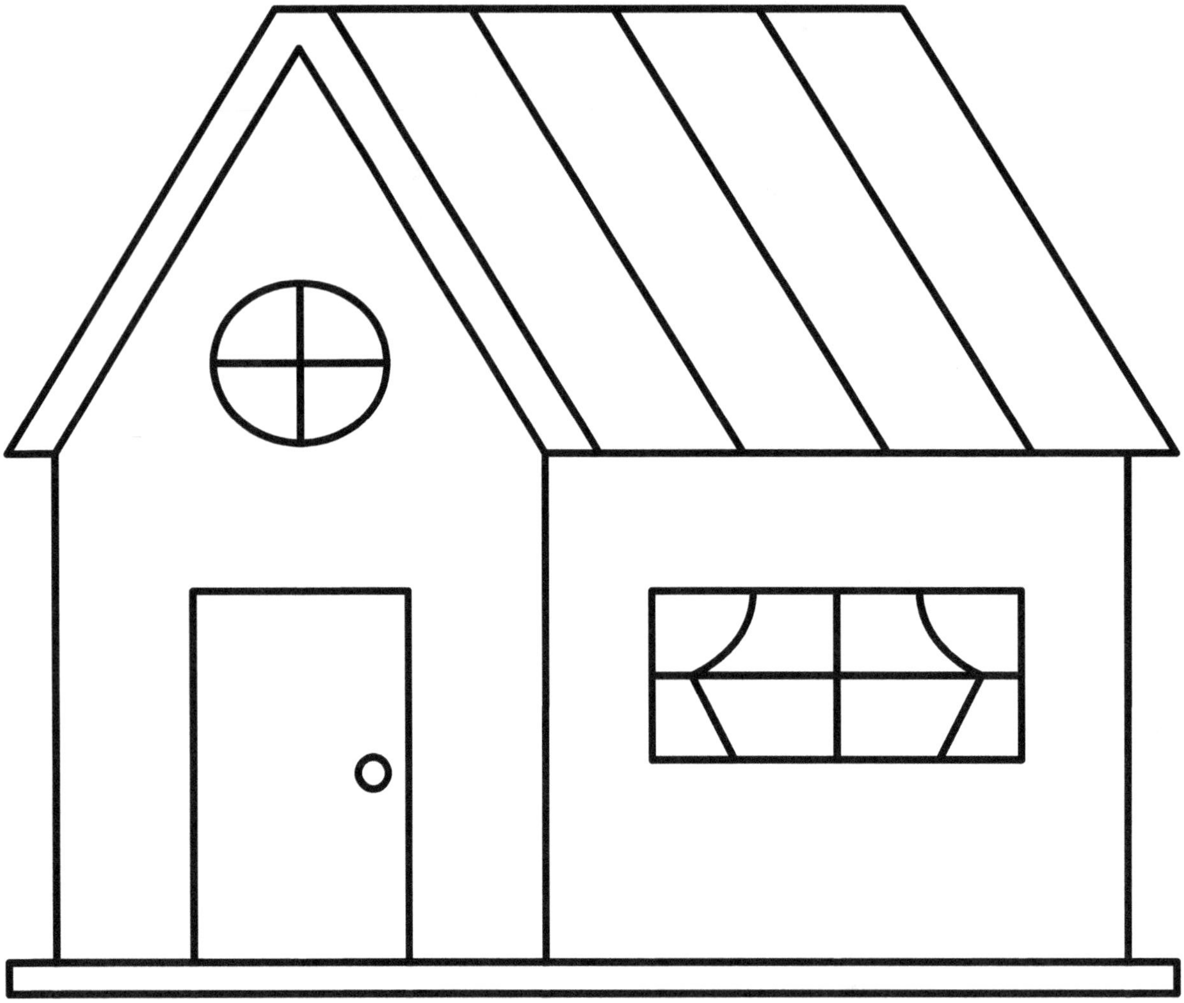

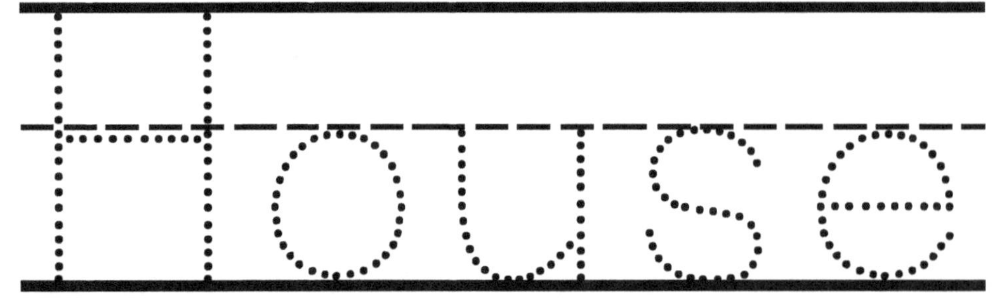

Score: ____________

Trace the letter

Trace the letter

Date: Score:

Alphabet A to Z

Color the drawing and trace the word

Ice Cream

Score: ______________

Trace the letter

Trace the letter

Date: Score:

Alphabet A to Z

Color the drawing and trace the word

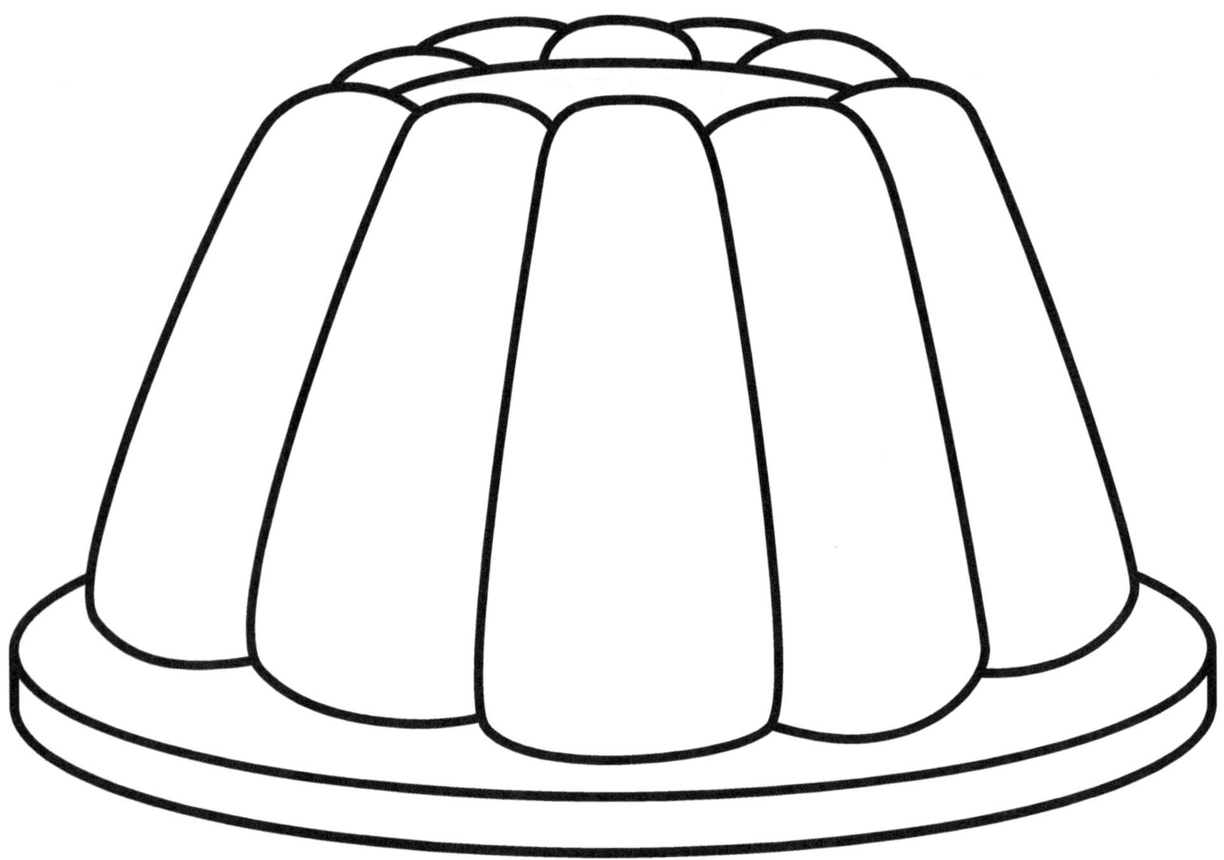

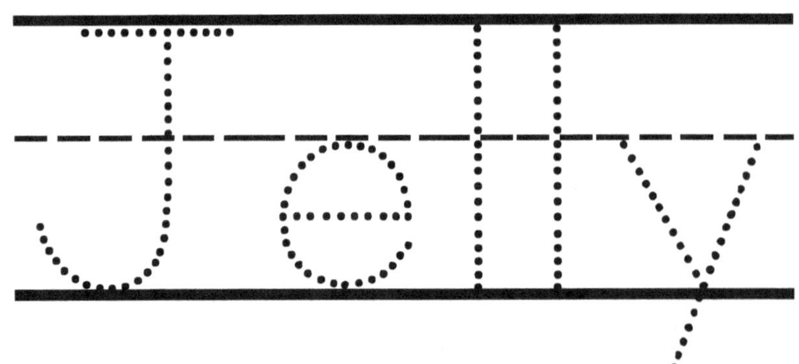

Score: ______________

Trace the letter

Trace the letter

Date: Score:

Alphabet A to Z

Color the drawing and trace the word

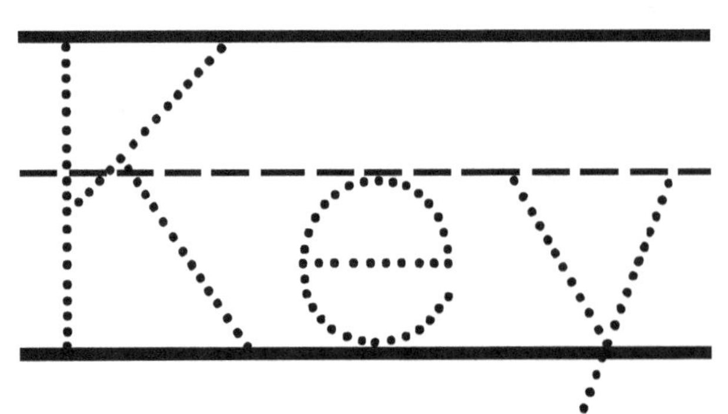

Score: ____________

Trace the letter

Trace the letter

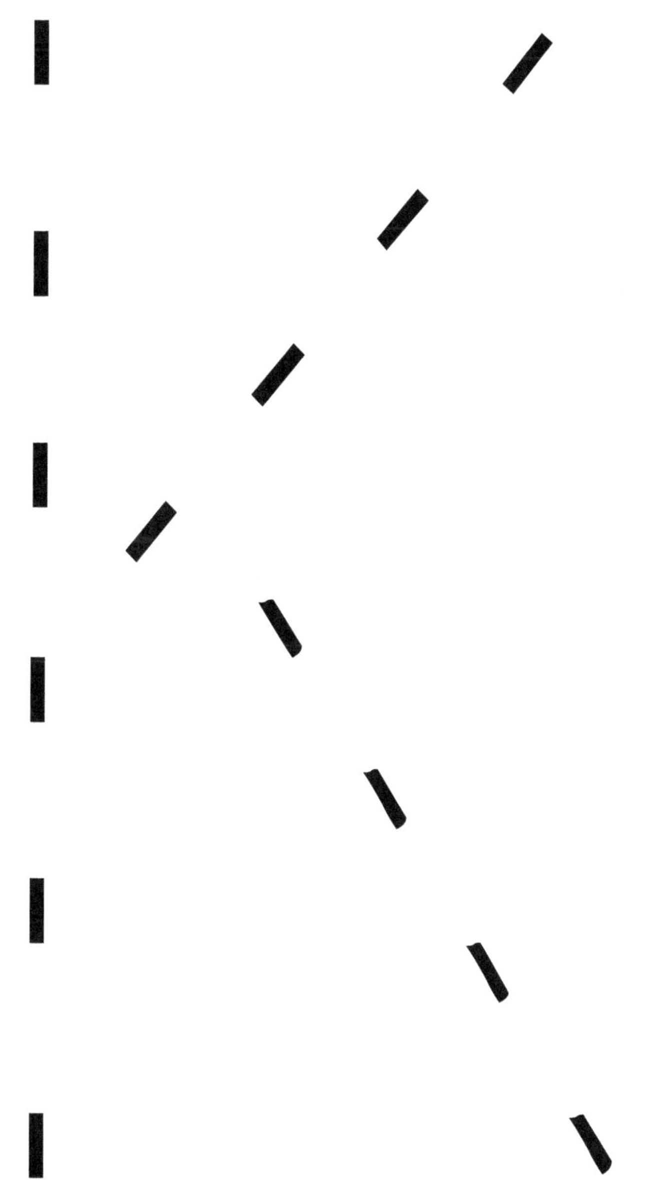

Date: Score:

Alphabet A to Z

Color the drawing and trace the word

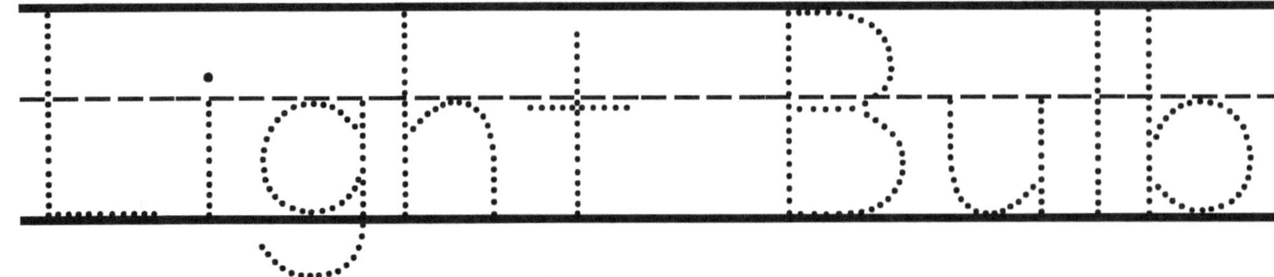

Score: ______________

Trace the letter

Trace the letter

Date: Score:

Alphabet A to Z

Color the drawing and trace the word

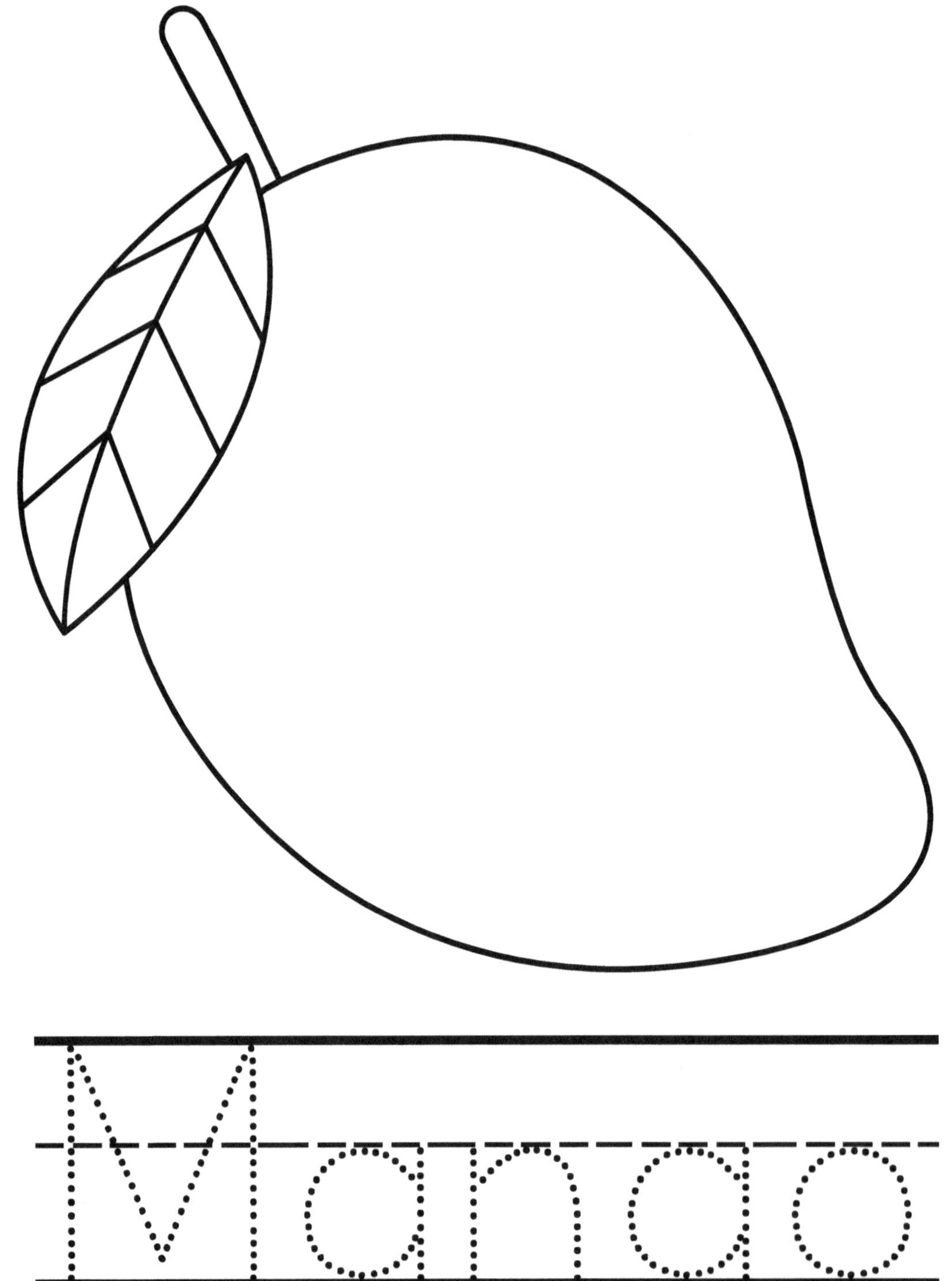

Mango

Score: ____________

Trace the letter

Trace the letter

Date: Score:

Alphabet A to Z

Color the drawing and trace the word

Notepad

Score: ______________

Trace the letter

Trace the letter

Date: Score:

Alphabet A to Z

Color the drawing and trace the word

Orange

Score: ____________

Trace the letter

Trace the letter

Date: Score:

Alphabet A to Z

Color the drawing and trace the word

Pinwheel

Score: ____________

Trace the letter

Trace the letter

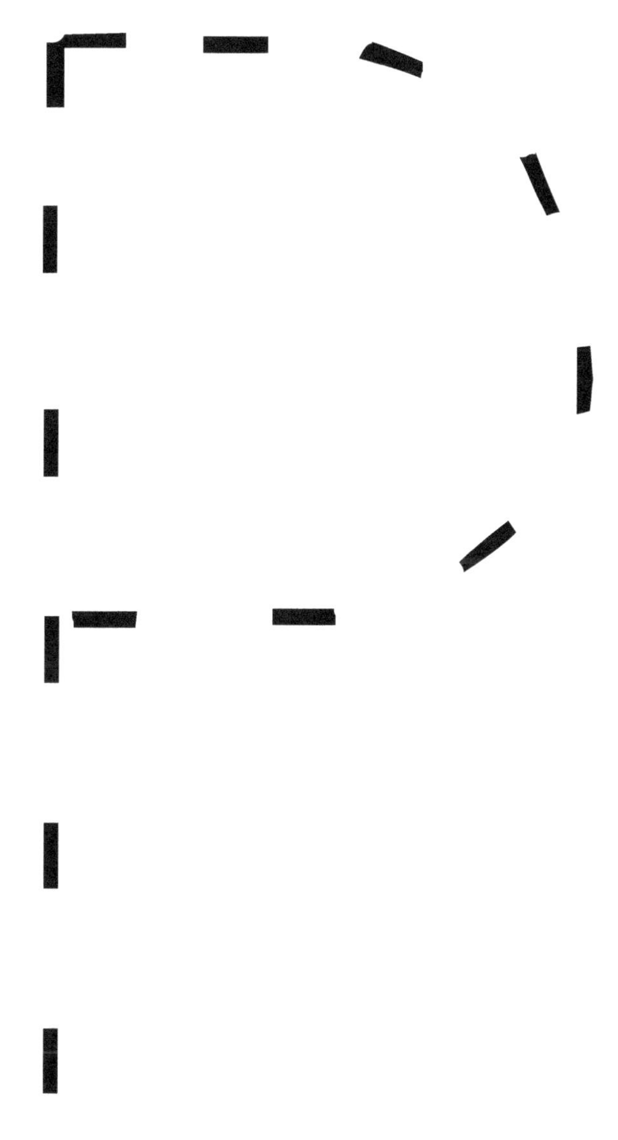

Date: Score:

Alphabet A to Z

Color the drawing and trace the word

Score: ______________

Trace the letter

Trace the letter

Date: Score

Alphabet A to Z

Color the drawing and trace the word

Rose

Score: ______________

Trace the letter

Trace the letter

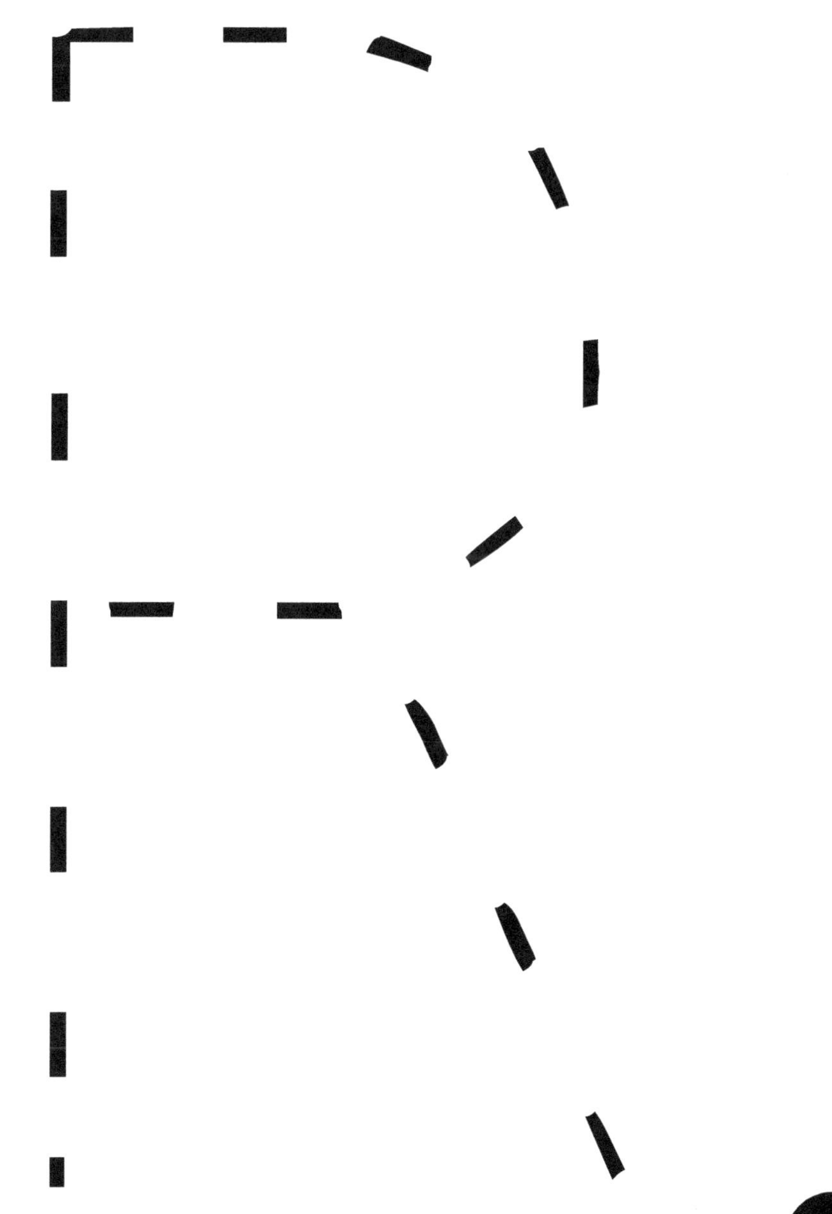

Date: Score:

Alphabet A to Z

Color the drawing and trace the word

Strawberry

Score: ______________

Trace the letter

Trace the letter

Date: Score:

Alphabet A to Z

Color the drawing and trace the word

Tree

Score: ______________

Trace the letter

Trace the letter

Date: Score:

Alphabet A to Z

Color the drawing and trace the word

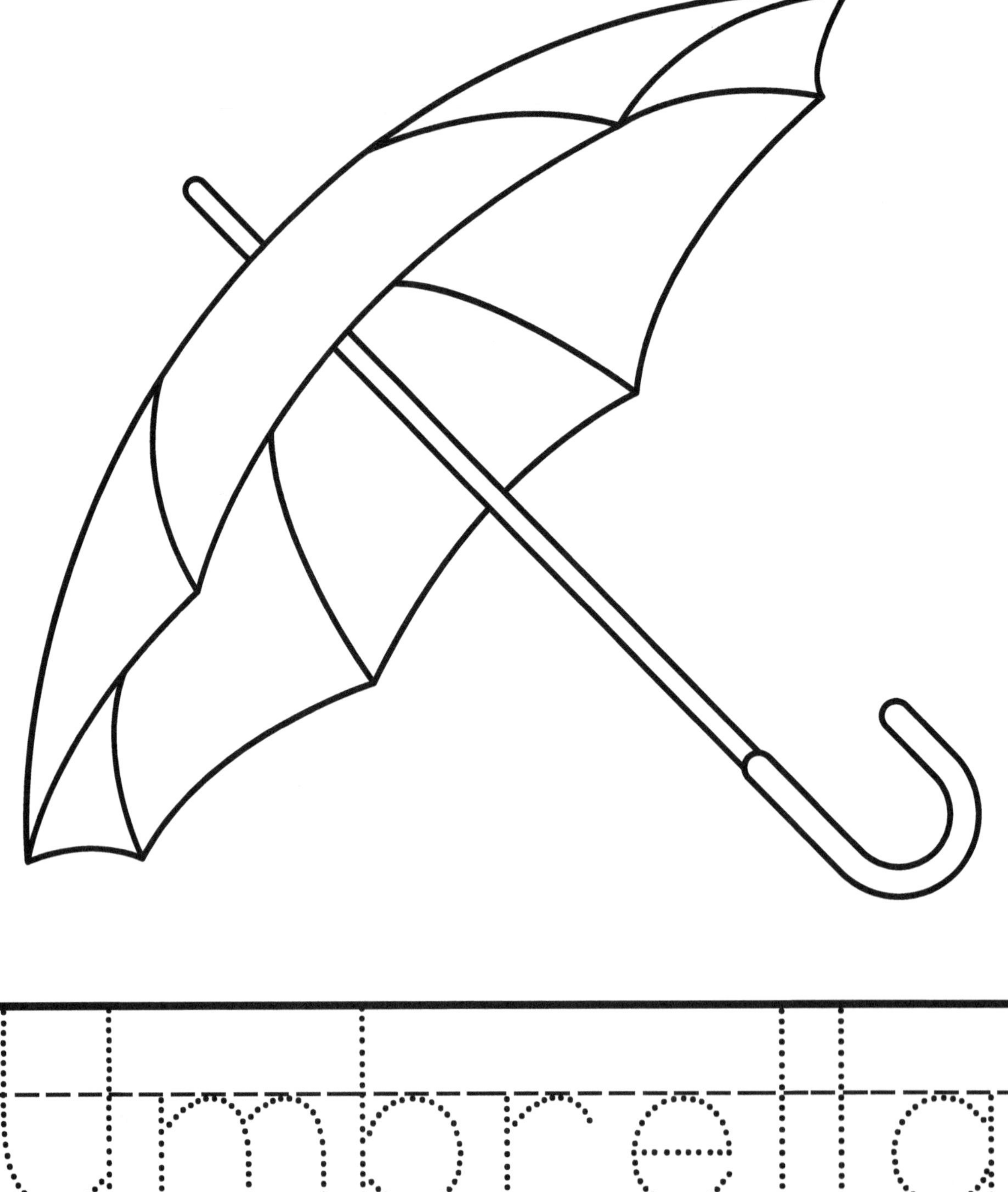

Umbrella

Score: ____________

Trace the letter

Trace the letter

Date: Score:

Alphabet A to Z

Color the drawing and trace the word

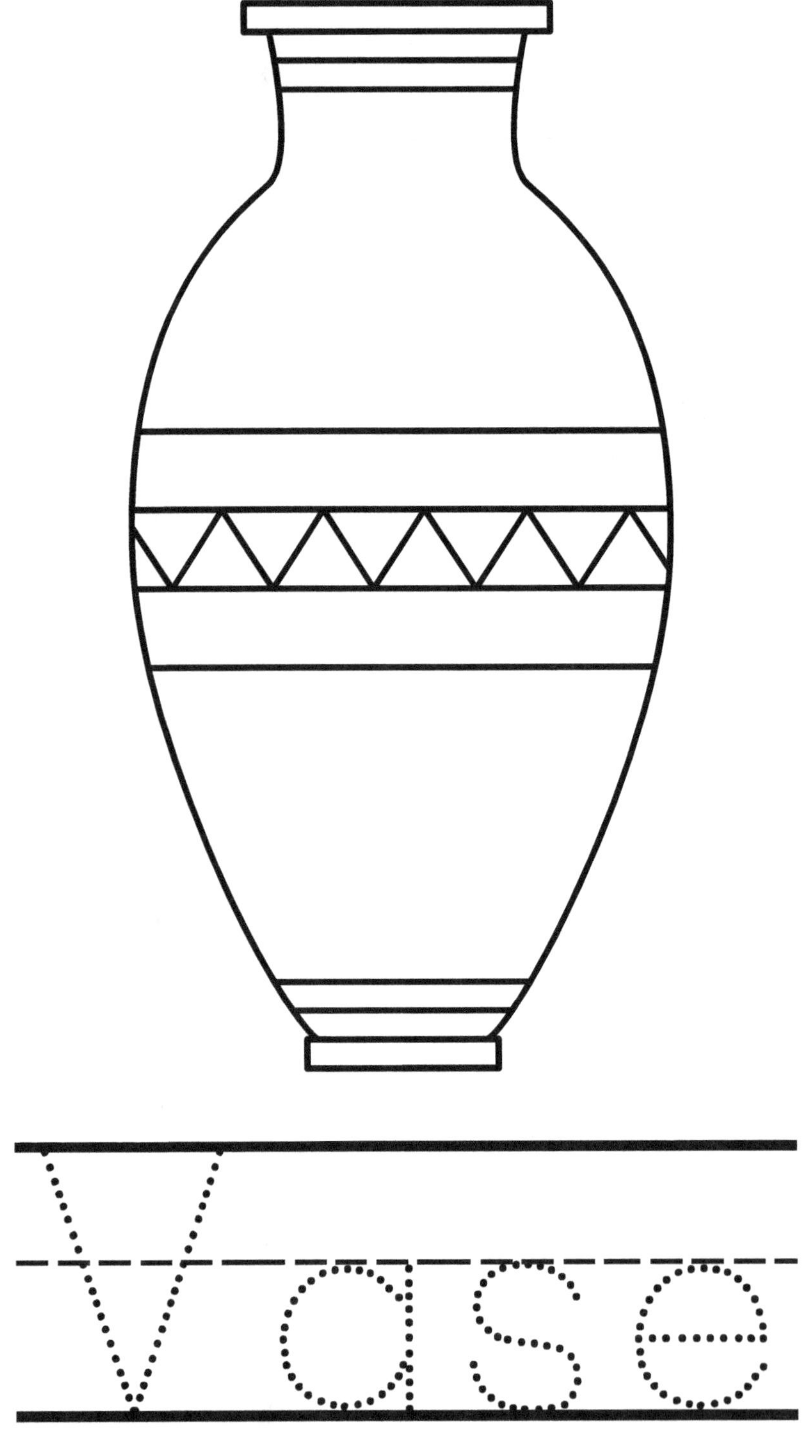

Score: ____________

Trace the letter

Trace the letter

Date: Score:

Alphabet A to Z

Color the drawing and trace the word

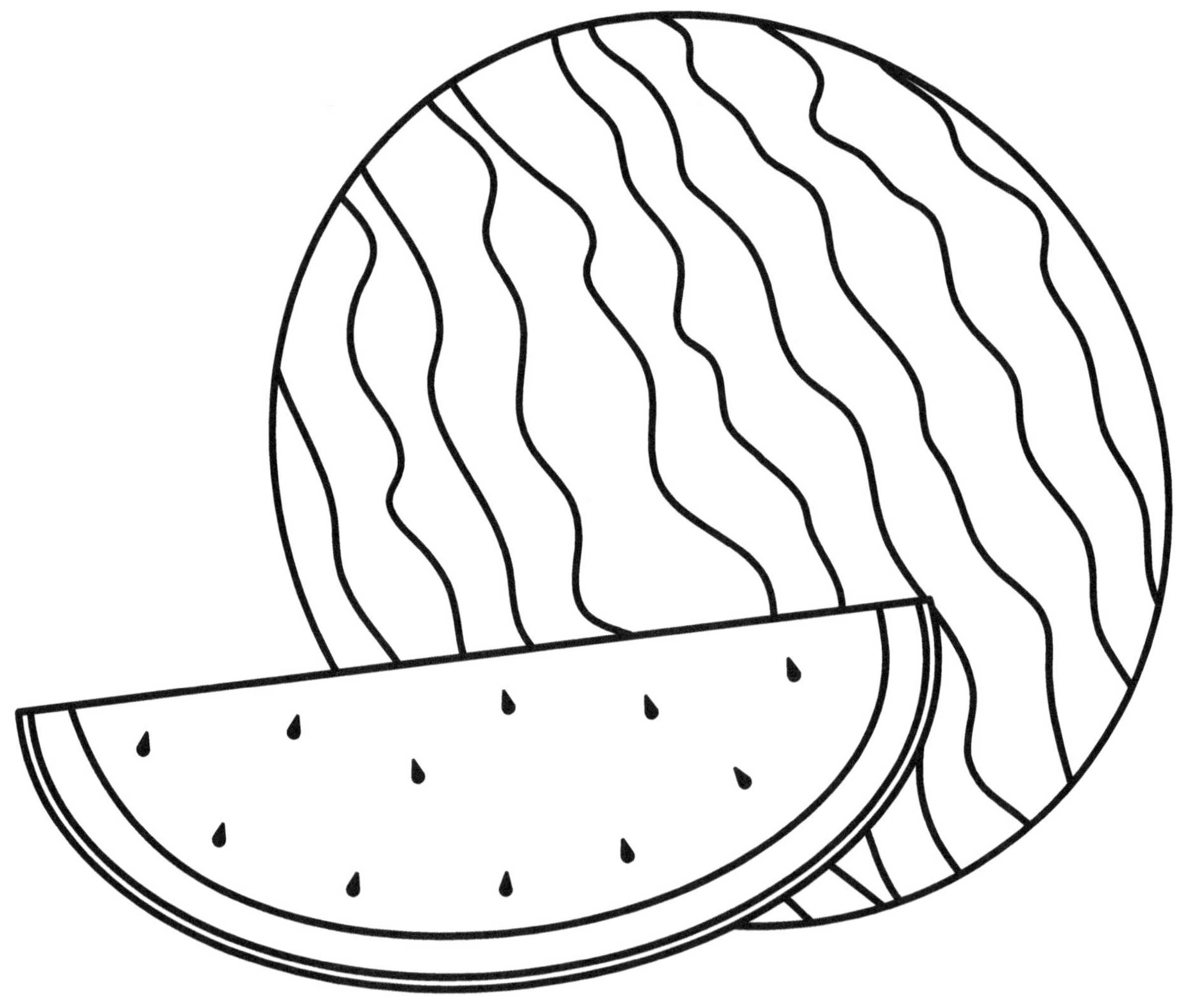

Watermelon

Score: ______________

Trace the letter

Trace the letter

Date: Score:

Alphabet A to Z

Color the drawing and trace the word

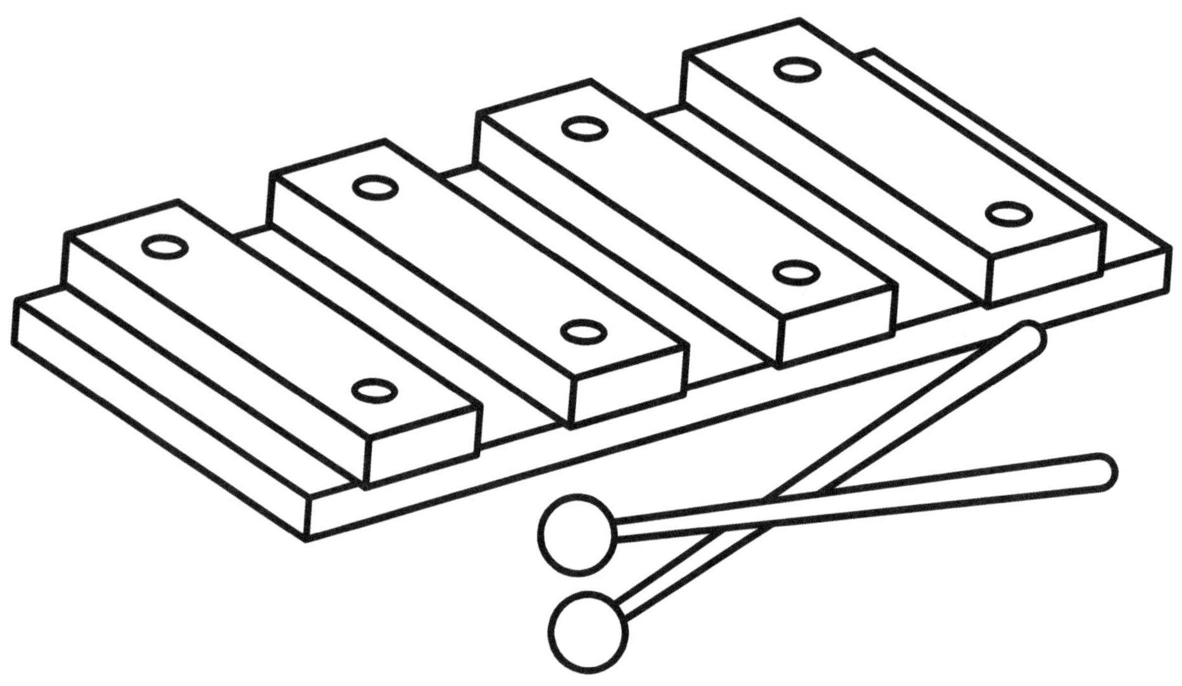

Xylophone

Score: ____________

Trace the letter

Trace the letter

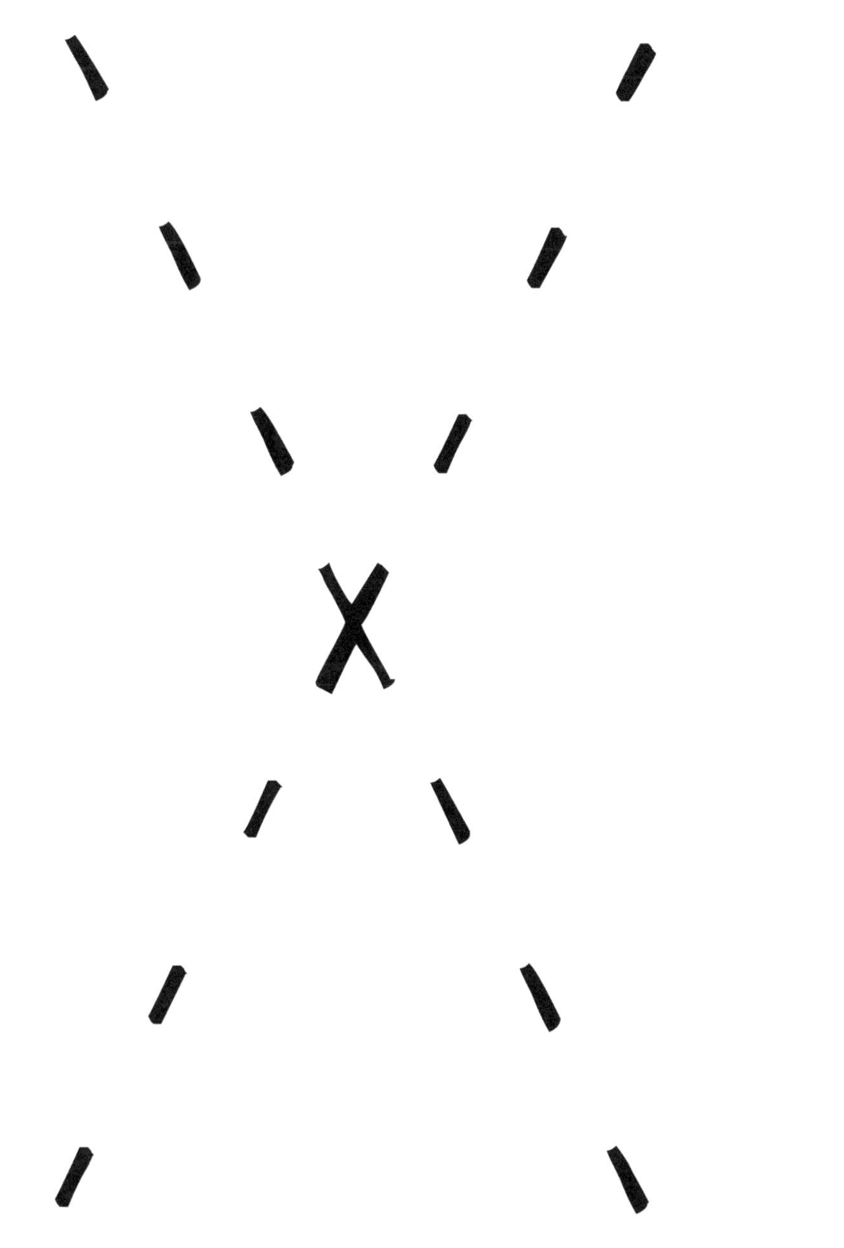

Date: Score:

Alphabet A to Z

Color the drawing and trace the word

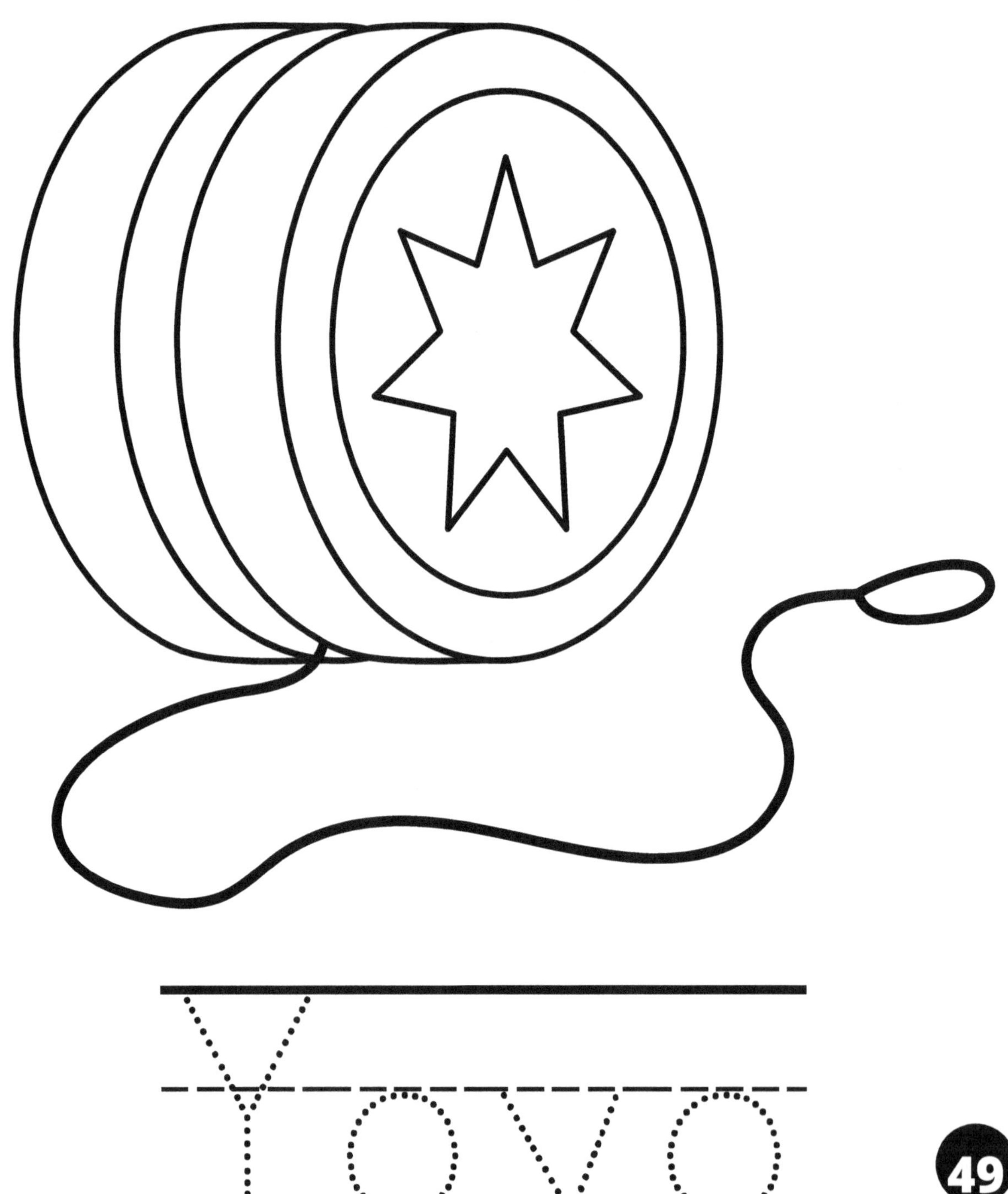

Score: ____________

Trace the letter

Trace the letter

Y

Date: Score:

Alphabet A to Z

Color the drawing and trace the word

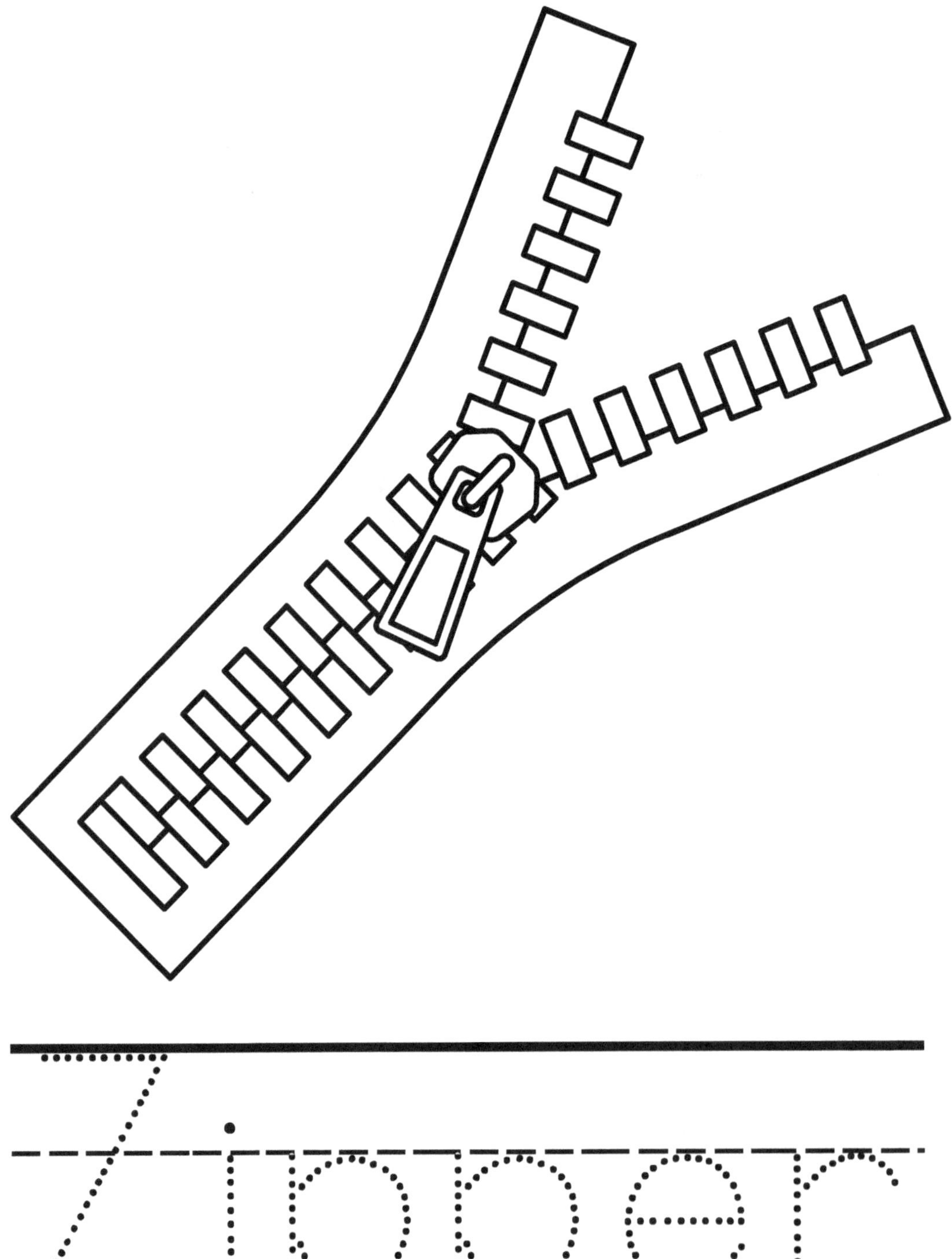

Zipper

Score: ____________

Trace the letter

Trace the letter

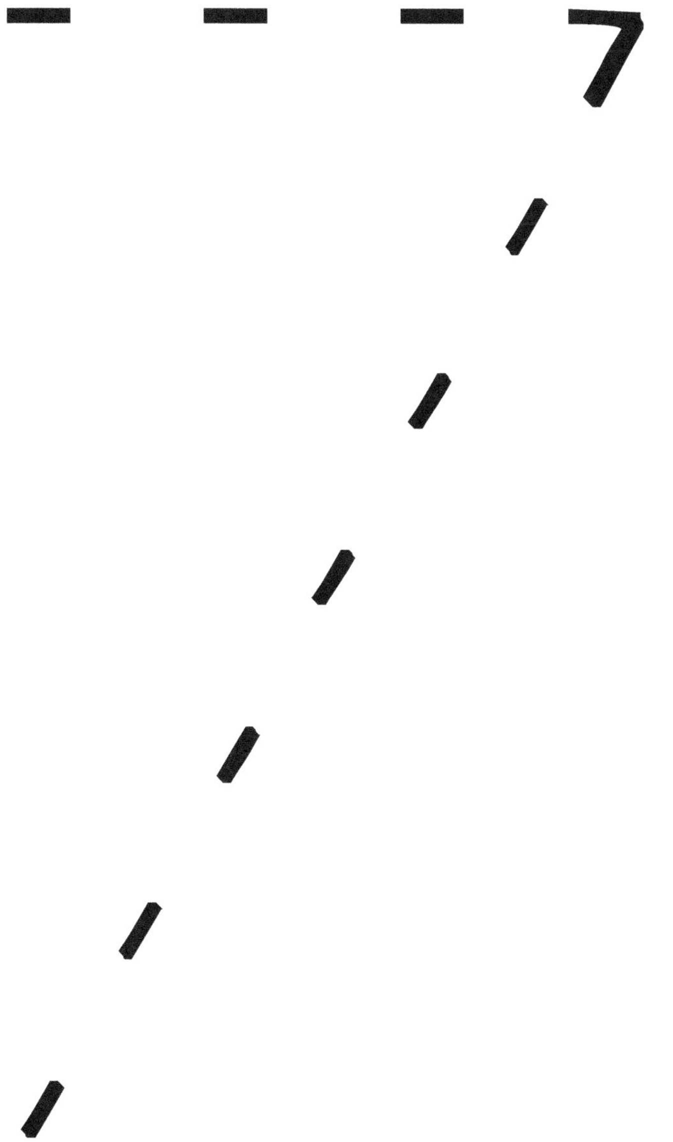

www.ingramcontent.com/pod-product-compliance
Lightning Source LLC
LaVergne TN
LVHW082259150826
845677LV00009B/1660